# THE ATLANTIC OCEAN

A TRUE BOOK

by
**David Petersen and
Christine Petersen**

Children's Press®

A Division of Scholastic Inc.

New York  Toronto  London  Auckland  Sydney
Mexico City  New Delhi  Hong Kong
Danbury, Connecticut

A reef octopus in
the Caribbean Sea

Reading Consultant
**Nanci R. Vargus, Ed.D.**
*Primary Multiage Teacher
Decatur Township Schools,
Indianapolis, IN*

The photograph on the cover
shows waves in the Atlantic
Ocean. The photograph on
the title page shows the
Atlantic coast at Acadia
National Park in Maine.

**Visit Children's Press® on the
Internet at:
http://publishing.grolier.com**

Library of Congress Cataloging-in-Publication Data

Petersen, David, 1946-
    The Atlantic Ocean / by David Petersen and Christine Petersen
        p.    cm. — (A True book)
    Includes bibliographical references and index.
    ISBN 0-516-22042-X      0-516-27312-4 (pbk.)
    1. Oceanography—Atlantic Ocean—Juvenile literature.  2. Atlantic
Ocean—Juvenile literature. [1. Atlantic Ocean. 2. Oceanography.]
I. Petersen, Christine.  II. Title. III. Series.
GC481.P43   2001
551.46'1—dc21                                            00-030666

# Contents

The Earth as seen from space

# Our Blue Planet

The first astronauts to see Earth from space called it "the Blue Planet." Shining blue water covers more than 70 percent of the globe.

Most of this water is contained in one vast, salty ocean. We divide this World Ocean into four great oceans: the

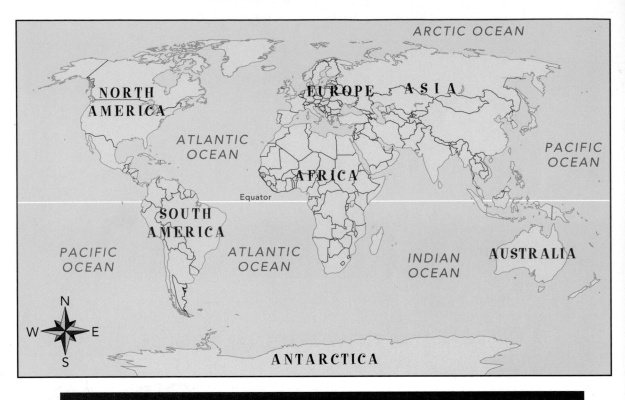

Atlantic, the Pacific, the Arctic, and the Indian.

The Atlantic covers almost 20 percent of our globe. It is the second largest of Earth's four oceans.

In shape, the Atlantic is long, narrow, and wavy—a bit like the letter S. In the north, near the North Pole, its waters lie frozen beneath thick ice. The warm equator runs across its middle.

Atlantic coastline along the eastern United States

In the south, its waters wash against the frozen continent of Antarctica, near the South Pole.

An ancient Greek legend tells of a king named Atlas, who ruled an island called Atlantis. On Atlantis, crops grew high, trees hung heavy with fruit, the rivers were leaping with fish, and everyone was wealthy.

But the people of Atlantis became greedy and stopped

**A map showing the mythical island of Atlantis**

giving thanks for the bless-
ings they had. This angered
the Greek god Zeus. He sent
an earthquake to destroy the

island, which sank into the Atlantic Ocean, never to be seen again.

The story of the Lost Continent of Atlantis is myth, not fact. Even so, it's a great way to remember how the Atlantic Ocean got its name: Atlas, Atlantis, Atlantic.

# Tides— Bound to the Moon

Atlantic coastline at low tide

The same place at high tide

Tides, the rise and fall of Earth's oceans, are caused by the moon. On the side of Earth facing the moon, the moon's gravitational pull causes the oceans to "bulge up" and draw away from shore, creating low tide. On the opposite side of the spinning Earth, the water also bulges outward, creating low tide there as well. These two high-water bulges move around the planet as the Earth turns. In between these areas, the moon's pull is weaker. Here the oceans "flatten out" and water moves onto shore, causing high tide.

# Oceans, Seas, Gulfs, and Rivers

Each of Earth's four oceans contain several seas. A sea is a small part of an ocean that lies near land. Among the Atlantic's seas are the Caribbean Sea, between Mexico and Cuba; the Weddell Sea, near Antarctica; and the Mediterranean Sea, between Europe and Africa.

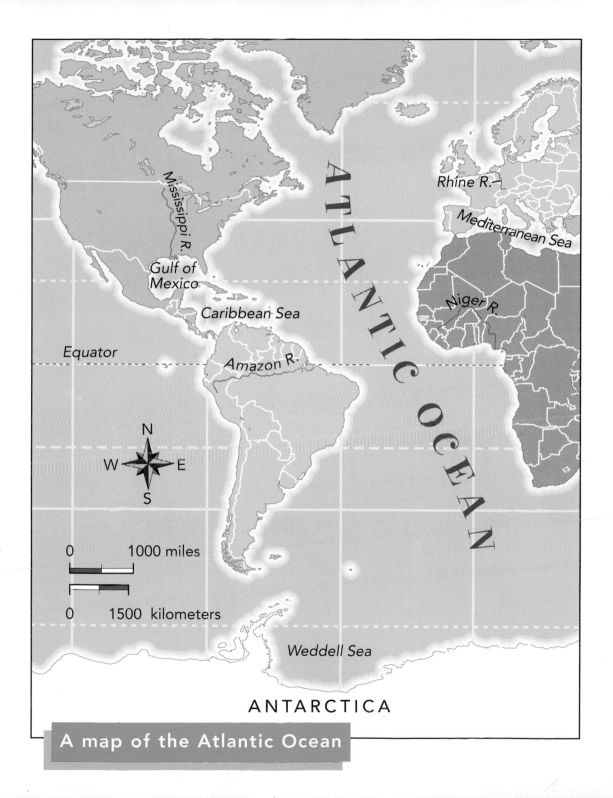

Mississippi R.

Rhine R.–

ATLANTIC OCEAN

Mediterranean Sea

Gulf of
Mexico

Niger R.

Caribbean Sea

Equator

Amazon R.

N
W   E
S

0     1000 miles

0     1500 kilometers

Weddell Sea

ANTARCTICA

A map of the Atlantic Ocean

Large areas of ocean that jut into the mainland are called gulfs. One example is the Gulf of Mexico, off the southern coast of the United States.

Oceans, seas, and gulfs get their water mostly from rainfall. But rivers also carry millions of gallons of fresh-water from land into the oceans every day. Major rivers that run into the Atlantic include the Mississippi in North

These photographs, taken from space, show where the Mississippi River (left) and Amazon River (right) feed into the Atlantic Ocean.

America, the Amazon in South America, the Niger in Africa, and the Rhine in Europe.

# The Atlantic Gulf Stream

Ocean currents are like rivers of warmer, colder, or saltier water that run through oceans. They affect the near-by weather. If the ocean water is warm, it makes the air above it warm.

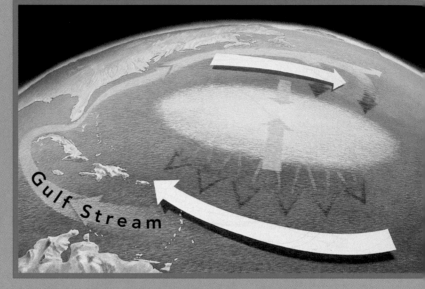

Gulf Stream

One of Earth's largest ocean currents is the Gulf Stream. This moving "river" of warmer water is up to 50 miles (80.5 kilometers) wide and travels up to 100 mi. (161 km) every day.

Forming in the Caribbean Sea, the Gulf Stream flows north through the Gulf of Mexico, up along the east coast of North America, and then west across the Atlantic. It helps warm the British Isles and northern Europe.

The Atlantic Ocean touches
69,482 mi. (111,820 km) of
shoreline. In surface area, this
second-largest ocean covers
about 41 million square miles
(107 million square kilometers).
Yet the greatest part of its
water lies hidden, far beneath
the rolling waves.

# Wonders of the Deep

The hidden mysteries of the ocean have always attracted adventurers and explorers. More than 2,000 years ago, Greek and Roman divers held their breath to explore the shallow waters of the Atlantic's Mediterranean Sea.

This mosaic shows how the ancient Romans were fascinated with the wonders of the Atlantic.

About 1,000 years ago,
seagoing adventurers from
Scandinavia, called Vikings,
sailed the open Atlantic in
small wooden ships. They

traveled as far as Greenland and North America.

By the 1520s, European explorers had sailed all the way around our big Blue Planet. But the murky depths of the Atlantic were still unexplored and completely unknown.

One of the first to map the ocean floor was Sir William Thomson. He sailed the northeastern Atlantic in the 1860s, measuring water

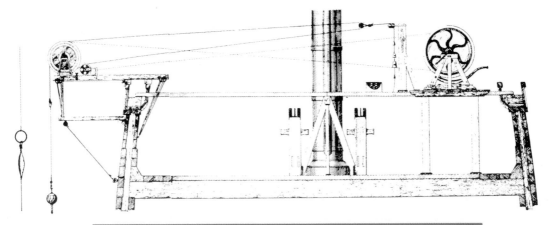

A diagram of the machine invented by Sir William Thomson to measure the depth of the Atlantic Ocean floor

depth with a long cable weighted with a lead ball.

In 1934, Charles William Beebe, an American scientist, became the first person to see the deep ocean and its creatures. His "bathysphere" was a hollow metal ball supplied with oxygen, searchlights, and a telephone. In his bathysphere, Beebe descended to the amazing depth of 3,028 feet (923 meters). That's the distance of ten football fields—

Charles William Beebe (in the middle) and his "bathysphere"

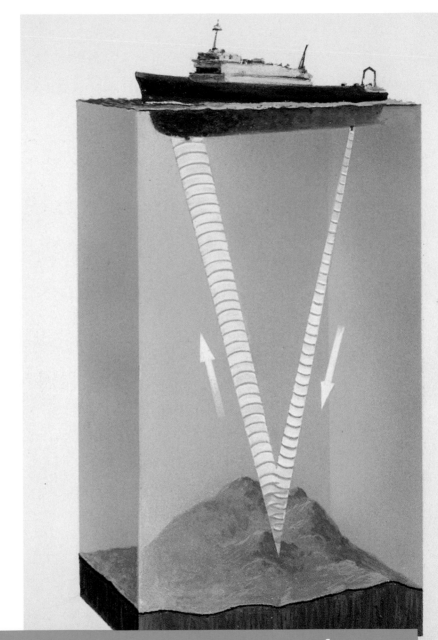

Today, oceanographers use sonar to map features of the ocean floor. They bounce sound waves off the seafloor and measure the time it takes for the sound waves to return to the surface as echoes.

far below the point where sunlight can reach.

Today, with the help of modern electronic instruments, scientists have measured and mapped nearly the entire ocean floor.

# The Ocean Floor

The Atlantic seafloor is divided into three major zones: the continental shelf; the continental slope; and the ocean floor, or abyss. The continental shelf is a shallow, gently sloping underwater "beach" that borders the continents. It extends about 250 mi. (402 km) off shore.

Coral reefs are found on some parts of the Atlantic's continental shelf.

In the Atlantic, the continental shelf's greatest depth is about 600 ft. (183 m). Beyond this, the continental slope dives steeply down to the ocean floor. Much of the ocean floor is flat, like a meadow. But there are

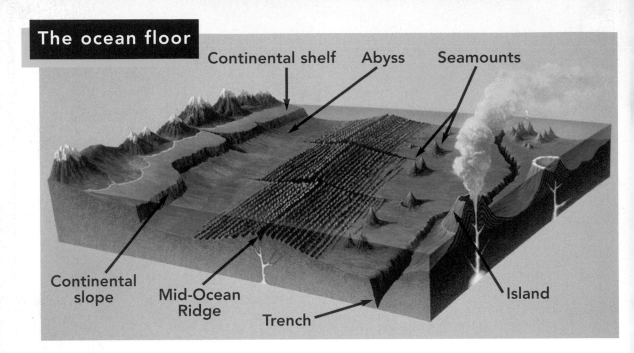

Continental shelf    Abyss    Seamounts

Continental slope

Mid-Ocean Ridge

Trench

Island

also underwater mountains and deep valleys.

The deepest point in the Atlantic Ocean is the Puerto Rico Trench, in the Caribbean Sea. This awesome underwater canyon plunges 28,374 ft. (8,648 m) below sea level.

# The Mid-Atlantic Ridge

ATLANTIC OCEAN FLOOR

The Mid-Atlantic Ridge is an underwater mountain range. It stretches north to south across the ocean floor, from Greenland almost to Antarctica. It is as wide as 1,000 mi. (1,609 km) in some places. Some of its peaks are tall enough to poke above the ocean surface, forming islands such as the Azores.

#  A Living Ocean

A great variety of living things call the Atlantic home—too many to name them all here. Pincushion-like sea anemones attach themselves to rocks near shore. During low tide, they curl up to avoid drying out. When the tide rises, the anemones

Sea anemones in the Atlantic

open like flowers to capture food with stinging "arms" called tentacles.

Lobsters have a hard shell covering their entire body. They use their long pincers to grab prey and to fight. They

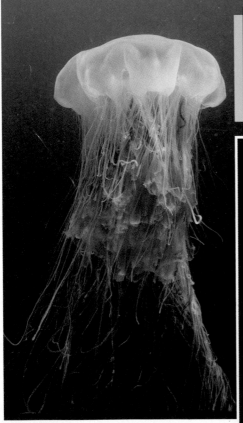

Caribbean spiny lobsters fighting (above), a lion's mane jellyfish (left), and a deep-sea anglerfish (below)

live along the North Atlantic continental shelf, hunting at night for
fish, crabs, and clams.

Lion's mane jellyfish float in
Atlantic waters from Florida to
the Arctic. Their round bodies are
pinkish-purple and up to 3 ft. (91
cm) wide, with tentacles dangling
as much as 100 ft. (30.5 m) below.

The deep, dark waters of the
Atlantic are home to such
strange creatures as the deep-
sea anglerfish. This fish has a
glow-in-the-dark "fishing lure"
dangling from its head. Its wide

jaws allow it to grab passing prey and swallow it whole.

Sea mammals, such as whales, dolphins, and seals, also live in the Atlantic. Blue whales are the largest animals in the world. These gentle giants grow up to 108 ft. (33 m) long and weigh more than 150 short tons (135 metric tons). Blue whales feed by scooping up huge mouthfuls of seawater and straining out millions of tiny, shrimplike creatures called krill.

The storm petrel is a small bird that spends its life searching the

A blue whale (above) and a storm petrel (right)

North Atlantic's choppy surface for food. Petrels drink saltwater and sleep floating on the open ocean. They come to shore only to nest, lay eggs, and raise their young.

# The Blue Atlantic and You

For centuries, boats have sailed the ocean blue. Today, the Atlantic is the world's most important water transportation route, connecting Europe, Africa, and the Americas.

Telephone cables laid across the Atlantic's floor allow people to talk and laugh together,

The Atlantic is an important transportation route for cargo ships.

even though they're thousands of miles apart.

The Atlantic Ocean, like the mythical island of Atlantis, is very generous to humans. Most importantly, it gives us food. Some of Earth's richest

Fishermen cleaning scallops near Newfoundland, Canada

fishing grounds are in Atlantic waters. These include Nova Scotia and the Grand Banks off Newfoundland, both in eastern Canada. Also, one-fourth of the world's remaining oil and gas reserves lie beneath the Atlantic's continental shelf.

An oil-exploration platform in the Gulf of Mexico

# A Modern Atlantis?

Despite its great size and power, however, the Atlantic Ocean is easily damaged. People harm it in many ways. Garbage is dumped from boats or washes out to sea from shore. Chemical poisons from farming and industry are carried by the rivers into ocean waters. And oil-pumping

People cleaning up an oil spill in San Juan, Puerto Rico

platforms, oil refineries, and supertankers spill tons of oil into the ocean, with deadly results.

All these poisons pollute the waters of the Atlantic and kill its plants and animals. At the same time, years of over-fishing have put some types of fish and whales at risk of extinction.

A polluted Atlantic-coast beach

Today, every living thing depends on the ocean for survival, directly or indirectly. Like the foolish people of the "Lost Continent of Atlantis," will we continue to take the ocean's gifts for granted until they, and we, are gone?

Perhaps not. Perhaps we can learn to protect the ocean, so that its wealth and beauty will last forever. If so, Earth will be an even healthier and lovelier place to live.

Waves breaking on a Bermuda beach

# To Find Out More

Here are some additional resources to help you learn more about the Atlantic Ocean:

 **Books**

Dipper, Frances. **Mysteries of the Ocean Deep.** Aladdin Books, 1996.

Johnson, Jinny. **Simon and Schuster's Children's Guide to Sea Creatures.** Simon and Schuster, 1998.

Petersen, David. **The Gulf of Mexico.** Children's Press, 2001.

Ricciuti, Edward R. **Ocean.** Benchmark Books, 1996.

Van Cleave, Janice. **Oceans for Every Kid.** John Wiley & Sons, Inc., 1996.

# Organizations and Online Sites

## Aquatic Network
*http://www.aquanet.com/*

A great site for general information about oceans. Includes "close-ups" on topics such as sharks, ocean exploration, and conservation.

## Gulf of Mexico Program
*http://pelican.gmpo.gov/edresources/kids.htm*

Information on pollution and conservation in the Gulf of Mexico, plus activities and links.

## New England Aquarium
Central Wharf
Boston, MA 02110
*http://www.neaq.org/*

A great place to learn about the marine life of the Atlantic Ocean. On its website, go into the LEARN section for at-home activities about the sea and its communities.

## Ocean Planet from the Smithsonian Institution
*http://seawifs.gsfc.nasa.gov/OCEAN_PLANET/HTML/search_educational_materials.html*

Includes lesson plans, at-home projects, and fact sheets about oceans, ocean exploration, and marine animals.

# Important Words

*canyon* deep valley with high, steep slopes

*continent* one of the major land masses of Earth

*equator* imaginary line around the middle of Earth

*extinction* the dying out of a type of animal or plant

*gravitational pull* force of attraction between two objects

*murky* hard to see through

*myth* traditional story

*oil refineries* places where oil is prepared for use by humans

*plunges* dips downward rapidly

*scavenger* animal that feeds off garbage and decaying matter

*supertanker* giant ship used for transporting oil

# Index

# Meet the Authors

David Petersen says he's learned a lot and had a lot of fun writing True Books for the past twenty years. And now that his daughter, Christine, is his writing partner, it's more fun than ever. David lives in Colorado.

Christine Petersen lives in Minnesota. She is an educator and biologist who studies North American bats. Chris inherited her father's love for the natural world, and has taught children about nature and science at museums, schools, and libraries.

Photographs ©: Corbis-Bettmann: cover (W. Cody), 38 (Raymond Gehman), 19 (Mimmo Jodice), 25 (Lawson Wood), 15 right; Dembinsky Photo Assoc./Susan Blanchet: 2, 27; Holiday Film Corp.: 4; Innerspae Visions/Mike Johnson: 35 top; Liaison Agency, Inc.: 7 (Eric Horan); 11, 20, 23 (Hulton Getty), 15 left (World Perspectives); National Geographic Image Collection: 16 (William H. Bond), 32 top (George Grall), 24, 28 (Lloyd K. Townsend); NOAA Department of Commerce: 22; Peter Arnold Inc.: 32 bottom left (Fred Bavendam), 32 bottom right (Norbert Wu); Photo Researchers: 11 top (Ted Clutter), 11 bottom (Ray Coleman), 1 (Adam Jones), 35 inset (Joyce Photographics), 41 (Andy Levin), 31 (Andrew J. Martinez), 42 (Gregory Ochocki), 37 (Chris Sharp); Stone: 43 (Martin Barraud), 17 (Jeremy Walker), 39 (Keith Wood).
Maps by: Joe LeMonnier